O
SEEKER
OF
PEACE

YOUR HEART KNOWS THE WAY

Ahmed
Mustafa

Hidayah
Publishers

O Seeker of Peace! Your Heart Knows the Way

ISBN (Paperback): 978-1-998843-46-6

Printed in the United States of America

CONTENTS

Preface

Do you sometimes feel as if your mind is a restless ocean, tossed by waves of worry, doubt, and endless "what-ifs"? Imagine yourself standing on the shore, watching the turbulent waters, longing for a sense of calm, a quiet place within. If you resonate with this feeling and if you've ever longed for the serene stillness that Rumi so eloquently describes, then you've picked up the right book.

Our modern lifestyle bombards us with distractions, demands, and a relentless pressure to perform. It's no wonder our minds feel like they're on an endless loop, replaying past mistakes, worrying about the future, and making it incredibly difficult to experience the peace we long for. This constant mental chatter can leave us feeling overwhelmed, anxious, and disconnected from the present moment—a feeling I know you're likely familiar with, especially as someone drawn to the wisdom of Rumi.

What if there were a path to navigate this inner turbulence, a way to find the tranquility that Rumi so beautifully expressed? In these pages, you'll discover practical tools and techniques inspired by Rumi's philosophical teachings. They can help you quiet your mind, connect with your inner wisdom, and find joy in the present moment. We'll explore how your thoughts are like fleeting visitors, how to manage the storms of your mind, and how to find that "peaceful field" within yourself—that oasis of calm that Rumi described.

This book isn't just a collection of ideas; it's a deeply personal exploration of how to apply the wisdom of Rumi to the challenges we face today. It involves drawing strength from the rich wellspring of Rumi's teachings and finding practical ways to incorporate them into our daily lives.

The pursuit of inner peace is a necessity. It's time to move beyond the endless cycle of overthinking and anxiety and begin living a life filled with purpose, joy, and genuine connection. You deserve a mind at peace. You deserve to experience the depth of meaning that life has to offer.

So, are you ready to begin this exploration of self-discovery and transformation? Let's begin, as Rumi would say, by welcoming your thoughts as guests. Let's turn to Chapter One, **"Thoughts Are Visitors; Welcome Them"**.

- Ahmed Mustafa

Chapter 1

THOUGHTS ARE VISITORS; WELCOME THEM

Our wakefulness fetters our spirits,

Then our souls are a prey to divers whims,

Thoughts of loss and gain and fears of misery.

They retain not purity, nor dignity, nor lustre,

Nor aspiration to soar heavenwards.

That one is really sleeping who hankers after each whim

And holds parley with each fancy.

— Rumi

"Out beyond ideas of wrongdoing and rightdoing, there is a field. I'll meet you there. When the soul lies down in that grass, the world is too full to talk about."

– Rumi (Translation by Coleman Barks)

This beautiful verse from Rumi speaks volumes about the peace that awaits beyond our constant mental chatter, beyond our judgments of what's right and wrong. It hints at a tranquil field where words are unnecessary, a place of serene stillness accessible when we quiet the restless mind. This chapter is all about grasping the essence of your thoughts, recognizing their immense power, and discovering how to find that peaceful field within yourself, even when your mind feels like a stormy sea.

Your mind is an incredibly powerful force. It can be your most steadfast ally or your harshest critic, capable of conjuring beautiful dreams or terrifying nightmares. It can elevate you to the heights of joy or drag you down into despair. The determining factor? Your thoughts. These thoughts, constantly flowing like a river, range from calm and gentle to turbulent and raging. They are a mix of memories, worries, plans, hopes, fears—the entire spectrum of human experience. Some are fleeting, like wisps of smoke, while others persist, like a catchy tune on repeat. But one thing is certain: they wield tremendous power.

The way you think shapes your perceptions, emotions, and actions. Your thoughts influence how you see yourself, the world around you, and your place within it.

They can be incredibly creative, inspiring you to write a book, start a business, or pursue a passion. However, they can also be incredibly destructive, fueling anxiety, depression, and self-sabotage. Like fire—they are a powerful force that can be used for good or ill. Fire can warm your home or burn it to the ground. The key is learning to control the flame, to harness the power of your thoughts for your benefit.

Interestingly, your thoughts aren't confined to your head. They have a tangible, physical impact on your body. When you experience a stressful thought, your body releases hormones like cortisol and adrenaline, preparing you for "fight-or-flight." Your heart rate increases, your muscles tense, and your breathing becomes shallow. This response is helpful if you're facing a real threat, like a charging bear. But when it's just your mind racing with worries about an upcoming presentation, it's not so helpful. Chronic stress, fueled by negative thoughts, can take a toll on your physical health, weakening your immune system, increasing your risk of heart disease, and even contributing to chronic pain. So, learning to manage your thoughts isn't just about improving your mental and emotional well-being; it's about improving your physical health, too. It's all interconnected.

Often, a feeling of discomfort arises from being trapped in a loop of negative thoughts. It's like being trapped in quicksand—the more you struggle, the deeper you sink. Your mind races with worries, doubts, and "what ifs," creating a sense of fear, dread, and overwhelm. It's important to keep in mind that this is a normal human experience. Everyone experiences it from time to time.

It's your body's way of signaling that something isn't right. But when this feeling becomes chronic, interfering with your ability to function in daily life, it's time to seek help.

"And when you are ill, it is He who cures you."

(Surah Ash-Shu'ara, 26:80)

This verse from the Quran offers solace and hope, reminding you that healing is always possible and that there is a source of comfort and recovery. It encourages you to seek help and have faith in the journey toward well-being, whether the ailment is physical or mental.

Rumi, the cherished Sufi poet, gives a deep understanding into the nature of thought and the importance of discovering tranquility surrounded by the clamor of life. His words, written centuries ago, are just as relevant today. He understood that our minds can be both a source of great wisdom and a source of great suffering.

In one Hadith, the Prophet Muhammad (peace be upon him) said, "There is a piece of flesh in the body if it becomes good (reformed) the whole body becomes good, but if it gets spoiled the whole body gets spoiled, and that is the heart." (Sahih al-Bukhari 52)

This Hadith highlights the crucial role of the heart—often considered the seat of emotions and intentions—in our overall well-being. When your heart is at peace, it positively impacts every aspect of your being.

Imam Ali, a prominent figure in Islamic history, once articulated, "The tongue is like a lion. If you let it loose, it will wound someone."

This saying can be extended to your thoughts as well. Uncontrolled thoughts, like an unleashed tongue, can cause harm. Learning to manage your thoughts is essential to preventing them from causing pain to yourself and others.

The Prophet Muhammad (peace be upon him) used to say, "O Allah! I seek refuge with You from worry and grief, from incapacity and laziness, from cowardice and miserliness, from being heavily in debt, and from being overpowered by (other) men." (Sahih al-Bukhari 6369)

Rumi reminds us that even our difficult thoughts, our "crowd of sorrows," are worthy of our attention. They are not enemies to be fought or suppressed, but messengers to be understood. He encourages us to approach them with curiosity and compassion. What are they trying to tell us? What can we learn from them? This doesn't mean wallowing in negativity, but rather engaging with our thoughts to understand their root and their message.

Rumi's Masnavi contains a story about a parrot and a grocer, which highlights how repetitive negative thoughts can lead to misinterpretations.

There was once a grocer who owned a beautiful green parrot, a gifted talker, and a melodious singer. One day, while the grocer was away, a cat ran into the shop, startling the parrot. In its frantic attempt to escape, the parrot knocked over bottles of almond oil, creating a mess. When the grocer returned and saw the chaos, he impulsively struck the parrot on the head. The poor bird, already feeling guilty, lost its ability to speak and sing. The grocer, realizing his mistake, was filled with remorse. He had not only lost his companion but also harmed his business. He tried to make amends, but the parrot remained silent. One day, a bald dervish walked into the shop, and the parrot suddenly spoke, asking, "Did you spill bottles of almond oil, too?" The parrot, you see, had mistakenly connected his own misfortune (caused by his actions) with the baldness of the dervish, thinking it was a similar punishment.

This story teaches a valuable lesson about the mind's tendency to make assumptions and jump to conclusions. Just like the parrot, we often misinterpret situations based on our limited perception. We create stories in our heads that may not be accurate, leading to unnecessary suffering. We react impulsively, like the grocer, without fully comprehending the consequences of our actions. This can create chaos, not only internally, but in our interactions with the world around us. It is crucial to pause, reflect, and avoid acting rashly based on impulses, especially when negative emotions are triggered.

Mindfulness

Mindfulness is a powerful tool for managing overthinking and anxiety. It involves paying attention to the present moment without judgment. It involves noticing your thoughts, feelings, and bodily sensations without getting caught up in them. It's like watching clouds drift across the sky—you observe them, but you don't try to control or change them. You simply allow them to be. When you practice mindfulness, you create space between yourself and your thoughts. You're no longer fused with them; you're observing them from a distance. This allows you to gain perspective, to see that your thoughts are not facts, but simply mental events. They are like waves on the ocean—they rise and fall, but the ocean remains.

You can incorporate simple mindfulness exercises into your daily life like these:

- Pay attention to the sensation of your breath as it enters and leaves your body. Notice the rise and fall of your chest or belly. Don't try to change your breath, just observe it. Or, bring your attention to different parts of your body, noticing any sensations without judgment. Start with your toes and gradually move up to the top of your head.

- You can practice mindful walking, paying attention to the sensation of your feet hitting the ground. Notice the movement of your body and the sights and sounds around you.

- Mindful eating involves paying attention to the taste, texture, and smell of your food. Savor each bite and eat slowly.

- You can even practice mindful listening, attentively listening to the sounds around you without getting caught up in your thoughts or judgments.

These exercises can help you cultivate a sense of presence and awareness, interrupting those negative thought spirals and bringing you back to the present moment. Quieting the mind is a practice, not a perfect state. Some days will be easier than others. On some days, your mind will be like a calm lake, reflecting the beauty of the sky. On other days, it will be like a stormy sea, tossing you about with waves of worry and doubt. Don't get discouraged. Just keep practicing. As you work on being more mindful, you'll start to notice changes. You'll become better at handling stress and your thoughts. You'll feel more connected to the present moment. You might not always be able to control what thoughts pop into your head, but you can change how you react to them.

Instead of trying to predict the future, concentrate on the now and investigate your inner domain. Be mindful of fear's influence and don't let it push you into impulsive decisions. Act with intention and courage, trusting the process of self-discovery. This path is about more than just stopping negative thoughts; it's about building a life full of purpose, joy, and peace by finding your own way to quiet the inner noise and connect with what truly matters.

As you learn to watch your thoughts without getting entangled, you gain a sense of control and begin to discover the peaceful field Rumi described—a place that's always within reach. This takes work, dedication, and consistent effort, but the rewards are immeasurable. You'll find a newfound sense of peace and clarity that transforms your entire outlook on life. Keep practicing, keep learning, keep growing. You are worth it, your well-being matters, and you deserve a peaceful mind. You got this.

Key Takeaways:

• Your thoughts significantly influence your emotions, perceptions, and even your physical health. They can be creative and inspiring or destructive and anxiety-inducing. However, you are not your thoughts. You are the observer of your thoughts and have the ability to manage them and choose how you respond.

• Getting caught in cycles of negative thinking, worrying, and ruminating can lead to feelings of anxiety, overwhelm, and even physical health problems. Recognizing these patterns is the first step to breaking free from them.

• Mindfulness practices help you to observe your thoughts without judgment, creating space between you and your thoughts. This allows you to see them as passing mental events rather than fixed realities, reducing their power over you.

~

Chapter 2

THE INNER CHAOS

Importune me not, for I am beside myself;

My understanding is gone, I cannot sing praises.

Whatsoever one says, whose reason is thus astray,

Let him not boast; his efforts are useless.

Whatever he says is not to the point,

And is clearly inapt and wide of the mark.

What can I say when not a nerve of mine is sensible?

Can I explain 'The Friend' to one to whom He is no Friend?

- Rumi

"Silence is the language of God, all else is poor translation."

- Rumi

Rumi understood that true connection, true understanding, often lies beyond words. It resides in the stillness, in the quiet spaces between our racing thoughts. But in our modern world, silence can be elusive. Our inner turmoil can make it difficult to hear that "language of God," the subtle whispers of wisdom that guide us toward peace and clarity. This is about learning to quiet that inner storm. It is about finding those moments of silence so you can begin to hear the deeper truths that reside within you. Just as a lake's surface must be still to reflect the sky clearly, our minds must find moments of calmness to reflect the wisdom that lies within.

This chapter builds on the last one, where we talked about how your thoughts can sometimes run wild. Now, we're going to focus on what you can do about it. You've started to understand how your thoughts work. You're beginning to see how that mental chatter can lead to anxiety and a general feeling of being overwhelmed. Now, it's time to learn some practical techniques to calm that restless heart of yours. This chapter is about giving you tools, real, usable tools that you can use every day.

When you're feeling anxious, it's like being caught in a storm. Your thoughts are racing, your heart is pounding, and your body feels tense. It's like being swept away by a strong current, struggling to stay afloat. The techniques we'll explore here are like anchors. They help you stay steady, even when things feel chaotic. They bring you back to the present moment, reminding you that you're safe, even when your mind is telling you otherwise.

Exercises

One effective way to ground yourself is through the **"5-4-3-2-1" exercise**. It's simple, it works, and you can do it anywhere. Here's how it works:

- Start by noticing **five** things you can see around you. It could be anything—a chair, a book, a spot on the wall, the light coming through the window, anything at all. Just take a moment to see your surroundings.

- Next, acknowledge **four** things you can touch. Feel the texture of your clothes, the weight of your phone in your hand, the floor beneath your feet. Feel into those sensations.

- Then, acknowledge **three** things you can hear. Maybe it's the hum of the refrigerator, birds singing outside, or the sound of your own breathing. Tune in to the sounds around you.

- Now, acknowledge **two** things you can smell. Maybe it's your morning coffee, the fresh air, or the scent of your lotion.

- Finally, acknowledge **one** thing you can taste. It could be the toothpaste in your mouth, a sip of water, or just the inside of your mouth.

This exercise helps shift your focus from your racing thoughts to your senses. It brings you back to the present moment. It's like hitting the pause button on your anxiety, giving your mind a chance to catch up. It's a way of saying, *"Okay, I'm here, I'm safe, and I'm in control."* This connects you to the physical world around you, which creates a pause from the whirlwind of thoughts in your mind.

Another powerful tool is your breath. It's always with you, available in any situation. When you're feeling anxious, your breath tends to get shallow and fast. This can make your anxiety worse. By consciously slowing down and deepening your breath, you can calm yourself down. It's like applying the brakes on your runaway thoughts.

Try this simple breathing exercise called **"Box Breathing"**:

- Think of your breath as a wave. When you inhale, the wave rises, filling your lungs with air. When you exhale, the wave recedes, releasing tension and stress. Ride that wave. Let it carry you to a place of stillness.

- Inhale slowly and deeply through your nose for a count of four.

- Hold your breath for a count of four.

- Exhale slowly through your mouth for a count of four.

- Hold your breath again for a count of four.

- Repeat this cycle for a few minutes.

You can do this anytime, anywhere. You don't need any special equipment or a quiet room. You can practice box breathing while you're waiting in line, sitting at your desk, or even lying in bed. It is a simple but powerful way to center yourself, even during a hectic day.

Here's another breathing technique called **"4-7-8 breathing"**:

- Inhale quietly through your nose for a count of four.

- Hold your breath for a count of seven.

- Exhale completely through your mouth, making a whooshing sound, for a count of eight.

- Repeat this cycle four times.

This is especially helpful for falling asleep, but you can use it during the day, too. You will find these breathing techniques especially effective when you start to feel that familiar sense of unease creeping in.

Mindful Movements

When your mind is racing, it's easy to feel disconnected from your body. You might feel like you're floating, or like your body isn't even there. Mindful movements can help you reconnect with your physical self. It grounds you in the present moment and reduces anxiety. This doesn't have to be anything complicated. It could be as simple as taking a walk around the block. Pay attention to the feeling of your feet on the ground, the wind on your skin, and the sights and sounds around you. Or you could try some gentle stretching or yoga. The point is to move your body in a way that feels good and helps you connect with your physical sensations. Pay attention to your body as you move. Notice the sensations in your muscles, the rhythm of your breath, and the way your body feels in space. There are no rules regarding mindful movement. You don't have to follow a specific routine or look a certain way.

This makes me think of an interesting story from Rumi's Masnavi, *"Deaf Man and His Sick Neighbor"*.

A man who was hard of hearing decided to visit his sick neighbor. He prepared what he would say, anticipating his neighbor's responses. But because he couldn't hear well, his conversation went hilariously wrong. He thought he was being kind and supportive, but his words were completely inappropriate for the situation. When he asked, "How are you feeling?" the sick man moaned, "I'm dying!" The deaf man cheerfully replied, "Thank God!" And when asked what he had eaten, the sick man answered, "Poison!" to which the deaf man responded, "Bon appétit!" Finally, when asked about his doctor, the sick man said, "Izrael, the Angel of Death!" The deaf man cheerfully said, "May he be blessed. His presence is always good news!"

This story highlights the importance of being truly present and attuned to the situation at hand. The deaf man was so caught up in his own preconceived notions that he failed to truly connect with his neighbor. His attempts at kindness were misguided and ultimately caused more harm than good. It also highlights the problem of relying on assumptions. The deaf man assumed he knew what his neighbor would say and how he should respond, rather than truly grasping the actual situation and responding accordingly. This teaches us the necessity of being fully present and aware when engaging with others.

As you start to incorporate the above-described techniques into your daily life, you'll begin to notice a shift. You might find yourself feeling more grounded, more centered, and more in control of your thoughts and emotions. It's important to keep in perspective that this is a process. There will be days when you feel like you're making progress, and there will be days when you feel like you're back at square one. That's okay. Be patient with yourself. Be kind to yourself. And keep practicing.

Contemplate the words of Prophet Muhammad (peace be upon him):

"The strong person is not the one who can wrestle someone else down. The strong person is the one who can control himself when he is angry." (Sahih al-Bukhari 6114)

This hadith emphasizes the importance of self-control, especially in relation to managing difficult emotions like anger.

One of Imam Ali's famous sayings is,

"The best deed of a great man is to forgive when he is able to take revenge."

This highlights the importance of forgiveness, both of others and of ourselves. When you learn to forgive, you free yourself from the burden of anger and resentment.

The Quran encourages patience and perseverance:

"O you who have believed, seek help through patience and prayer. Indeed, Allah is with the patient."

(Surah Al-Baqarah, 2:153)

This verse reminds you that you're not alone in your struggles and that patience is a virtue that will be rewarded.

It won't always be easy. There will be times when you feel like giving up. But keep going. You are stronger than you think. You have within you the capacity to overcome any challenge. It's about learning to navigate the ups and downs of life with grace and resilience, and ultimately, finding peace within yourself, even when things around you are chaotic. It's about finding freedom from the grip of anxiety and overthinking, and connecting with something larger than yourself, whether that's God, the Universe, or simply the present moment.

The tools you've learned in this chapter are just the beginning. As you continue, you'll discover new techniques, new insights, and new ways of coping with the challenges that life throws your way. You are capable of amazing things. You have within you the power to create a life of peace, joy, and fulfillment.

Key Takeaways:

• You are not alone in your struggle with anxiety and overthinking. Many people experience these challenges, and there are tools that can help.

• Grounding techniques, like the '5-4-3-2-1 exercise', can help you anchor yourself in the present moment and reduce anxiety. They help you connect with your senses and remind you that you're safe.

• Your breath is a powerful tool for managing anxiety. By slowing down and deepening your breath, you can calm your nervous system and quiet your mind.

• Mindful movement can help you reconnect with your body and reduce anxiety. It's about moving in a way that feels good and helps you connect with your physical sensations.

• This is a journey, not a destination. Be patient with yourself, be kind to yourself, and keep practicing.

~

Chapter 3

THE PRESENT

Yea like cups on the surface, till they are. filled;

And when filled, these cups sink into the water.

The ocean of Reason is not seen; reasoning men are seen;

But our forms (minds) are only as waves or spray thereof.

Whatever form that ocean uses as its instrument,

Therewith it casts its spray far and wide.

– Rumi

"If you are depressed, you are living in the past. If you are anxious, you are living in the future. If you are at peace, you are living in the present."

- Lao Tzu

This quote, while not from Rumi, beautifully captures the essence of what we'll be exploring in this chapter. It's a powerful reminder that true peace is found in the present moment. In the previous chapters, we talked about the whirlwind of thoughts that can take over your mind and explored ways to calm that storm. Now, let's explore what happens when the storm begins to settle, when you find those moments of stillness, those pockets of peace in the everyday chaos. That, my friend, is where the magic happens—where you discover the gift of presence.

Presence means truly being here, in this moment, right now. Not lost in the past, not worrying about the future, but fully present in the only moment that truly exists. Think about the last time you were really present. Maybe you were playing with your child, completely absorbed in their laughter and joy. Maybe you were walking in nature, feeling the sun on your skin and the breeze in your hair. Or maybe you were simply savoring a delicious meal, fully appreciating each bite. In those moments, you weren't thinking about your to-do list or worrying about something that happened yesterday. You were fully there, in the present moment.

That's what we're aiming for. That's the gift we're trying to unwrap. It's not about eliminating all thoughts, but about learning to choose which thoughts we give our attention to. It involves shifting our focus from the endless chatter of the mind to the richness of our sensory experience. This is a practice, and it can change your life.

One of the most effective ways to cultivate presence is to tune into your senses. Your senses are your direct connection to the present moment. They're your anchors to reality. When your mind is spinning, your senses can bring you back to the here and now. Let's try a little experiment.

- Take a deep breath. Close your eyes for a moment, if you're comfortable doing so. Now, slowly open your eyes and look around you. What do you see? Notice the colors, the shapes, the textures. Take it all in. Don't label things or judge them, simply observe.

- Now, shift your attention to the sounds around you. What do you hear? The gentle hum of the refrigerator? The chirping of birds outside? The sound of your own breath? Let the sounds wash over you, like waves on the shore.

- Next, become aware of your body. Feel the weight of your body in the chair, the texture of your clothes against your skin, the temperature of the air. Notice any sensations you feel without judgment. Just observe. Now, take a deep breath and notice the scents around you. Maybe it's the aroma of your morning coffee, the fresh air from an open window, or the subtle fragrance of a nearby flower.

- Finally, if you have a drink or a piece of food nearby, take a sip or a bite. Pay attention to the taste, the texture, the sensation as you swallow. Savor it.

This is presence. This is what it feels like to be fully engaged in the present moment. And it's something you can practice anytime, anywhere. No special equipment or quiet place is necessary. You can practice presence while washing the dishes, walking to work, or even sitting in a meeting. It is about bringing your full attention to whatever you are doing, right here, right now.

Gratitude

Another powerful way to cultivate presence is through the practice of gratitude. When you focus on what you're grateful for, you shift your attention away from what's lacking or what's causing you stress. You start to appreciate the good things in your life, no matter how small. But gratitude is more than just a feel-good practice; it actually rewires your brain. Studies have shown that practicing gratitude activates the medial prefrontal cortex, a part of the brain associated with learning and decision-making. It also releases dopamine and serotonin, neurochemicals that make us feel good and promote social bonding.

In other words, gratitude isn't just about feeling thankful; it's about actively training your brain to focus on the positive, which can lead to reduced stress, improved relationships, better sleep, and greater resilience. It's a way of acknowledging the good, even when things are tough. By consistently practicing gratitude, you're not just changing your mindset; you're changing your brain, making it easier to experience joy, contentment, and a deeper sense of connection. You begin to see that even during challenges, there is always something to appreciate: the roof over your head, food on your plate, the love of family and friends, or simply the miracle of being alive and experiencing this incredible world.

Keep a gratitude journal. Each day, write down three to five things you're grateful for. This simple practice can have a deep impact on your overall well-being, reducing stress and promoting a sense of inner peace. Spend time in nature. Nature has a way of bringing us back to ourselves. Take a walk in the park, sit by a tree, and listen to the birds sing. Let the beauty of the natural world soothe your soul.

Try this: Every morning when you wake up, before you even get out of bed, think of three things you're grateful for. They can be big things, like your health or your loved ones, or small things, like the warmth of your blanket or the sound of the rain outside. As you go about your day, continue to look for things to be grateful for. The more you practice, the easier it will become. Think of a time when someone unexpectedly showed you kindness. Maybe a stranger held the door for you, a friend offered a helping hand, or a family member surprised you with a thoughtful gesture. How did that act of kindness make you feel? Did it brighten your day? Did it make you feel appreciated and loved? This simple feeling is the power of gratitude in action. When we take the time to appreciate the good in our lives, even the small things, we open ourselves up to a more positive and fulfilling experience.

True gratitude goes beyond simply listing things we appreciate. It's a shift in our being, a recognition of the source of all blessings. Sometimes, the things we are most grateful for are not what we initially expect. We might even find ourselves feeling thankful for the challenges and even the difficult people in our lives, recognizing that they have helped us grow and learn. Rumi illustrates this idea in a story about a holy man who prayed for sinners.

In a small town, there lived a holy man known for his unusual prayers. He prayed fervently for sinners, for those who had strayed from the right path. People were confused by this. Why didn't he pray for the good and righteous?

One day, someone asked him, "Why do you always pray for those who do wrong?"

The holy man smiled and replied, "Because their mistakes have been my greatest teachers. When I saw them stumble, it made me more determined to walk a righteous path. Their errors have strengthened my faith and deepened my compassion. I am grateful for the lessons they have unknowingly taught me. That is why I pray for them, that they too may find their way."

This reminds us that sometimes, the greatest lessons come from the most unexpected sources. Even the wrongdoings of others can serve as reminders of the good we should follow.

This holy man's unusual prayers stemmed from a place of deep gratitude. He recognized that even the negative actions of others had played a role in his spiritual development. He was thankful for the lessons he had learned by observing their mistakes, for they had strengthened his own faith and drawn him closer to God. This perspective invites us to consider whether we, too, can find gratitude in unexpected places. Can we look back on difficult experiences in our lives, the mistakes we have made, or even the difficult people we have encountered, and find something to be thankful for? Perhaps a lesson learned, a strength gained, or a new perspective acquired.

This kind of gratitude, a gratitude for unexpected blessings, can help us find peace and meaning during life's ups and downs. It helps us to be present, to accept what is, and to trust that there is a larger purpose at work, even when we can't see it.

Rumi often used stories like these to teach thoughtful lessons about life. He saw the sacred in the ordinary, the divine in the everyday. He wrote, "Today, like every other day, we wake up empty and frightened. Don't open the door to the study and begin reading. Take down a musical instrument. Let the beauty we love be what we do. There are hundreds of ways to kneel and kiss the ground."

What a beautiful invitation! Rumi is telling us to stop getting lost in our heads, in our studies, in our worries. He's urging us to wake up to the beauty and wonder of the present moment. He's encouraging us to find joy in the simple things, to let the beauty we love be what we do. He says there are "hundreds of ways to kneel and kiss the ground." This isn't about a specific religious practice, instead, discovering your connection to something greater and expressing thanks for the gift of life. It might be through prayer, meditation, spending time in nature, creating art, or simply taking a moment to appreciate the beauty of a flower. Find what resonates with you and make it a regular practice.

The Quran emphasizes the importance of mindfulness and remembrance of God:

"O you who have believed, remember Allah with much remembrance. And glorify Him morning and evening."

(Surah Al-Ahzab, 33:41-42)

This verse encourages a state of constant awareness and connection with the Divine, which is a core aspect of presence.

The Prophet Muhammad (peace be upon him) said,

"Worship Allah as if you see Him, for if you don't see Him, He surely sees you." (Sunan Ibn Majah 64)

This hadith highlights the importance of being mindful of God's presence in every moment, which enhances our ability to be present.

Cultivating presence is a daily practice. It's like building a muscle. The more you work at it, the stronger it becomes. Here are some helpful tips for you:

- Start small. You don't have to meditate for hours each day to experience the benefits of presence. Start with just a few minutes each day.

- Find a quiet place where you can sit comfortably and close your eyes. Focus on your breath, or on a specific object, or on a mantra. Be patient. Your mind will wander. That's okay. It's what minds do. When you notice your thoughts drifting, gently bring your attention back to your breath or to your chosen object of focus. Don't judge yourself. Just keep practicing.

As Ibn Ata'Allah Al-Iskandari said,

"The reality is that you have nothing but the present, so be mindful of it."

Incorporate mindfulness into daily life. Bring a sense of presence to everyday activities like washing dishes, taking a shower, or walking the dog. Pay attention to the sensations, the sights, the sounds, the smells. Be fully present in whatever you're doing.

Disconnect from Technology

Give yourself regular breaks from your phone, computer, and other devices. The constant stimulation that these devices provide can make it challenging to be fully present in the moment. Therefore, it is indispensable to carve out some time for yourself to step away from the digital world and create space for quiet reflection and connection with yourself and others. By doing so, you allow your mind to rest, rejuvenate, and regain focus. These breaks can be as short as a few minutes or as long as a few hours, depending on your needs and schedule.

If you're struggling to cultivate presence on your own, consider seeking support from a therapist, counselor, or spiritual advisor. They can provide guidance and support as you navigate this path.

Be patient. Life is messy. It's full of ups and downs, joys and sorrows, successes and failures. It's not about trying to create a perfect life, free from pain or discomfort. It's about learning to navigate the messiness with grace and resilience, and finding beauty in the imperfections and meaning in the struggles.

As Rumi wisely said, "The wound is the place where the Light enters you." Your challenges, your disappointments, your heartbreaks—they are not obstacles to be overcome, but opportunities for growth and transformation. They are the places where the light can enter you, illuminating your path and guiding you toward a deeper understanding of yourself and the world around you. We are all in this together, stumbling, learning, and growing as we go.

Being present also means accepting things as they are, without resistance. It means letting go of the need to control everything and trusting that there is a larger plan at work. This can be challenging, especially when things aren't going our way. But when we learn to accept the present moment, even the difficult parts, we free ourselves from a lot of unnecessary suffering. It is about finding peace within yourself, regardless of what is happening around you. It's about recognizing that you are not your thoughts, and you are not your circumstances. You are something much greater, something much deeper.

As a part of the universe, you are a divine spark with infinite potential. And when you connect with that part of yourself, when you truly cherish the present moment, you open yourself up to a world of possibilities. You discover a peace that surpasses understanding, a joy that is unshakeable, and a love that knows no bounds.

So, take a deep breath. Feel the ground beneath your feet. Listen to the sounds around you. Notice the sensations in your body. Be here, now. This moment is all there is. And in this moment, you are exactly where you need to be.

Key Takeaways:

- Presence is about being fully engaged in the present moment, rather than being lost in thought about the past or future.

- Tuning into your senses is a powerful way to cultivate presence. It anchors you in the here and now.

- Gratitude shifts your focus from what's lacking to what's abundant, fostering a sense of appreciation for the present moment.

- Cultivating presence is a daily practice that requires patience and persistence.

- Valuing the present moment, even the difficult parts, allows you to find peace within yourself and connect with something larger than yourself.

- This journey is about learning to truly live, discovering a richness and depth to life that you never knew existed.

~

Chapter 4

YOUR INTUITION

Like this spade, our hands are our Master's hints to us;

Yea, if ye consider, they are His directions to us.

When ye have taken to heart His hints,

Ye will shape your life in reliance on their direction;

Wherefore these hints disclose His intent,

Take the burden from you, and appoint your work.

He that bears it makes it bearable by you,

He that is able makes it within your ability.

Accept His command, and you will be able to execute it;

Seek union with Him, and you will find yourselves united.

- Rumi

"Your heart knows the way. Run in that direction."

- Rumi

This powerful verse from Rumi encapsulates the essence of this chapter. It's about that inner knowing, that gut feeling, that subtle voice within each of us that guides us toward our true path. But in a world that often prioritizes logic and reason, learning to trust this inner wisdom can be a journey in itself. So, let's explore this a little deeper. We are going to focus on rediscovering your inner compass, learning to listen to its subtle guidance, and developing the courage to follow where it leads.

For too long, our society has placed logic and reason on a pedestal, often dismissing intuition as something unreliable or even irrational. But what if I told you that your intuition is just as valuable, if not more so, than your rational mind? Think of it this way: your logical mind is like a computer, processing information and making decisions based on data. It's great for analyzing facts and figures, but it can sometimes miss the bigger picture. It can get caught up in the details and lose sight of the overall context.

Your intuition, on the other hand, is like a wise elder. It draws upon a deep well of experience, both conscious and unconscious, to provide you with insights that go beyond logic. It's that gut feeling you get when you meet someone new, that sense of knowing when something is right or wrong, that inner nudge that tells you to take a chance or walk away. It is not about ignoring logic, but about recognizing that there are other ways of knowing, ways that are just as valid and important.

Intuition speaks to us in whispers, in subtle sensations, in dreams, and in moments of quiet reflection. It's a language of the heart, not the head. And the more you learn to listen to it, the more you'll find that it's a powerful and reliable guide. Science is now beginning to catch up with what mystics and sages have known for centuries: intuition is real, and it's powerful. Studies have shown that our brains are constantly processing information below the level of conscious awareness, picking up on subtle cues and patterns that we're not even aware of. This information is then relayed to us through our intuition, often in the form of a gut feeling or a sudden insight.

Neuroscience research has identified specific areas of the brain that are involved in intuitive processing, including the insula, the anterior cingulate cortex, and the ventromedial prefrontal cortex. These areas work together to integrate information from different parts of the brain, including the emotional centers, to provide us with a sense of knowing that bypasses conscious thought. So, when you get that "feeling" about something, it's not just random. It's your brain's way of communicating important information to you. It is your internal guidance system at work.

The first step in trusting your intuition is learning to listen to it. This can be challenging, especially if you've spent a lifetime ignoring or dismissing those inner nudges. But like any skill, it takes practice. One way to start tuning into your inner wisdom is to pay close attention to your body and its subtle signals. Your body is a powerful receiver of intuitive information, constantly providing feedback about the world around you. When you're faced with a decision or a situation, notice any physical sensations that arise. Do you feel a tightness in your chest, perhaps a knot in your stomach, or a sudden headache? These could be signs that something isn't quite right. On the other hand, a feeling of lightness, a sense of warmth spreading through your chest, a tingling sensation, or a gut feeling of certainty can indicate that you're on the right path. Some people experience intuition as a quiet knowing, a sense of peace, or even a subtle energy shift within their body. The key is to start paying attention to these cues, however subtle they may be.

Let's try a simple exercise right now to help you connect with your intuition:

- Find a comfortable place to sit or lie down. Feel free to close your eyes and take several deep breaths.

- Now, bring to mind a decision you need to make, big or small. It could be something as simple as what to have for dinner or as significant as a career choice. Hold that question in your mind and then turn your attention to your body. Notice any sensations that arise. Is there a feeling of tension or ease? A sense of expansion or contraction? Do you feel drawn toward one option or repelled by another? Don't try to analyze these sensations, simply observe them. What is your body telling you? Spend a few minutes with this practice and write down any insights that emerge. This is your intuition speaking to you, offering its wisdom.

Intuition vs Impulses

Now, you might be skeptical about this whole idea of intuition. You might be thinking, "Isn't this just wishful thinking or random feelings?" And that's a valid point. It's important to acknowledge that not every feeling or sensation is a message from your intuition. Sometimes, a stomach flutter is just a sign of indigestion, and a headache might just mean you need more water. This is where discernment comes in. Learning to trust your intuition is also about learning to differentiate it from other internal signals, like fear, anxiety, or impulsive desires. Intuition tends to be calm, persistent, and aligned with your values, while impulses are often fleeting, driven by immediate gratification, and can lead to regret.

For example, an impulsive urge to quit your job in the heat of the moment is likely driven by frustration, whereas a persistent intuitive feeling that you're meant for a different path, a feeling that brings a sense of peace and purpose, is worth exploring. Think of it like this: impulses are often loud and demanding, while intuition is more like a gentle whisper. It takes practice to distinguish between the two. You can start by noticing patterns. When have you followed your gut and it led to a positive outcome? When have you ignored it and regretted it later? For instance, have you ever had a gut feeling about a person that turned out to be accurate? Or a sense that you should take a different route home, only to find out later that there was an accident on your usual path? These are everyday examples of intuition at work. Keep track of such incidents.

Impulses are often driven by our ego's desires for immediate gratification or avoidance of discomfort. They are reactive and can often lead to choices that we later regret. Intuition, on the other hand, is connected to a deeper, wiser part of ourselves. It's proactive, guiding us toward choices that are aligned with our long-term well-being and our authentic selves. With practice, you'll become more attuned to your body's signals and better at distinguishing between the whispers of your intuition and the shouts of your impulses or fears. The more you listen to and act upon your intuition, the stronger and clearer it will become.

Make time for recognizing your intuitions each day, even if it's just for a few minutes. Sit quietly, close your eyes, and focus on your breath. Let go of your thoughts and simply be present. Jot down any gut feelings, hunches, or dreams that seem significant in a journal. When faced with a decision, ask yourself, "What feels right to me?" or "What is my intuition telling me?" Don't overthink it. Just notice the first thought or feeling that comes to mind. And perhaps most importantly, practice trusting your intuition in small ways. Start with small decisions. Trust your gut when choosing what to eat, what to wear, or which route to take to work. The more you practice trusting your intuition in small ways, the easier it will become to trust it in bigger matters.

Now, let's visit a story from Rumi's Masnavi, "The Three Fish," to illustrate the power of heeding that inner voice.

Three beautiful fish lived in a clear pond at the foot of a mountain. The water was so clear, you could see the bottom. They'd always lived there, safe from harm, until one day some men walked by and saw them. The men, excited by their find, rummaged through their things and found an old, tangled fishing net. They started to untangle it, making noise as they worked. The three fish watched, not understanding what the men were doing.

But one fish felt a strange feeling, a sense of unease. It felt like it needed to leave the pond, even though there was no obvious danger yet. It trusted this feeling and decided to go. Knowing the others wouldn't want to leave their familiar home, it didn't say anything. It bravely leaped into the fast-flowing stream that ran out of the pond, ending up in the boundless sea where it felt truly free. It could swim without circling the same space, and was happy it had listened to its instincts.

The men were still busy with their net. The second fish realized it should have followed its wise friend. It quickly stopped blaming itself. Knowing it was too late for regrets, it pretended to be dead. It flipped onto its back and floated, still, on the water. The men, thinking it was dead, threw it onto the bank. Quickly, it flipped away and swam as fast as it could, never wanting to see a human again.

The third fish, however, panicked. It thrashed around trying to escape, making itself easy to catch. The men threw the net over it and quickly had it cooking over a fire. As it burned, it thought about how it should have gone with its wise friends to the sea. It knew it was too late and wished it had listened and left the pond behind.

This tale, though simple, speaks a lot about intuition. The first fish, attuned to its inner voice, acted decisively and found a better life. It didn't wait for undeniable proof of danger; it trusted the subtle prompting of its intuition. We, too, can learn to recognize and heed these inner nudges, these whispers of wisdom that guide us towards our own 'vast sea' of possibilities. How often do we, like the third fish, ignore our intuition, only to find ourselves caught in the nets of regret? This story serves as a gentle reminder to tune in to that inner knowing, that 'gut feeling' that often knows the way, even when our logical mind is still untangling the net.

This Quranic verse beautifully underscores the truth about the nature of inner peace when we do the right thing:

"He is the One Who sent down serenity upon the hearts of the believers so that they may increase even more in their faith. To Allah 'alone' belong the forces of the heavens and the earth. And Allah is All-Knowing, All-Wise."

(Surah Al-Fath, 48:4)

This verse from the Quran highlights the blessing of 'sakina', the divine tranquility bestowed upon the hearts of believers. It is within this state of inner peace that our connection to Allah (God) is strengthened, and we become more receptive to the subtle guidance of intuition. A believer may sometimes hesitate to take decisions based solely on intuition, those gut feelings or inner nudges that seem to defy logic. However, when anchored in the belief that Allah is "All-Knowing, All-Wise," a sense of peace settles upon the heart, allowing them to trust in a wisdom that transcends their own.

This is not to say that intuition should replace reason or careful consideration. Rather, it suggests that when we are at peace, grounded in our faith, our intuition can serve as a powerful compass, guiding us towards choices that are aligned with a larger, divine plan. By surrendering our anxieties and trusting in God's infinite wisdom, we create space for our intuition to speak clearly, illuminating the path ahead. This inner guidance, coupled with sincere intention and effort, can lead us to make decisions, both big and small, that resonate with our deepest values and ultimately bring us closer to our true purpose. It is a harmonious interplay between our inner knowing and our faith in the All-Knowing, an alignment that unfolds with grace and serenity when we are at peace within ourselves and connected to the Divine.

The Prophet Muhammad (peace be upon him) once gave this powerful advice:

"Consult your heart. Righteousness is that about which the soul feels at ease and the heart feels tranquil. And wrongdoing is that which wavers in the soul and causes uneasiness in the breast." (Hadith 27, 40 Hadith an-Nawawi)

In simple terms, your heart knows what's truly right, even when your mind is confused. The Prophet (peace be upon him) is telling us to listen to that inner knowing. He says that when something is good and righteous, it'll make your soul feel calm and your heart feel peaceful. It's like a feeling of everything being in the right place. But when something is wrong, even if it looks good on the outside, your soul will feel uneasy, and your heart will feel a bit shaky. That shaky feeling is your inner compass, your intuition, trying to tell you, "Hold on, this isn't the right path."

Sometimes, what seems like the smart choice, or the choice that'll get you ahead quickly, isn't what's best for you in the long run. That's when you need to listen to your heart. Your heart, that inner voice, is connected to something bigger, something wiser. And when you learn to trust that feeling, to trust your intuition, you'll find yourself making choices that lead to real peace and happiness, the kind that lasts. It is like the Prophet (P.B.U.H) said, consult your heart and you will know what is right.

Imam Ali once said, "The most trustworthy of people is one who is not swayed by passion, nor deceived by his desires." This emphasizes the importance of being guided by inner wisdom rather than by fleeting emotions or desires, which can often cloud our judgment and lead us away from our intuitive knowing.

When you follow your intuition, you open yourself up to new possibilities, to unexpected adventures, and to a deeper connection with yourself and the world around you. You begin to live a life that is more authentic, more aligned with your true purpose, and more fulfilling.

Here's a fun little intuition test you can do. When faced with a decision, try this: Flip a coin. Heads for one option, Tails for the other. As soon as the coin lands, notice your immediate gut reaction. Were you hoping for a particular outcome? This can reveal your true preference, even if it seems not the logical choice.

Learning to trust your intuition is an exercise of deepening your connection with yourself, with your inner wisdom, and with the divine intelligence that flows through all things. As you continue on this path, remember to be patient with yourself. There will be times when you doubt your intuition, when you make mistakes, and when you feel lost. That's okay. It's all part of the process. Trust that your inner compass is always guiding you, even when you can't see the path ahead. Trust that you have within you all the wisdom you need to navigate life's challenges and create a life that is truly meaningful and fulfilling.

Recognize yourself as not just a physical being, but a spiritual being as well. You are intrinsically connected to a larger, divine whole. A world of possibilities opens up when you trust your intuition and connect with your inner self.

And as we move forward, let us carry the wisdom of Rumi with us: "Let yourself be silently drawn by the stronger pull of what you really love." This is the essence of trusting your intuition. It's about letting yourself be drawn by the love that resides within you, the love that connects you to your true self, to others, and to the divine. It is about finding your own unique way of connecting with that inner wisdom and allowing it to guide you on your journey. Trust that inner voice. It knows the way. It is your compass, your guide, your inner knowing. Learn to listen to it, to trust it, and to follow where it leads. You are capable of amazing things when you learn to trust yourself.

So, take a deep breath. Close your eyes for a moment. And ask yourself: What is my intuition telling me right now? What is my heart longing for? What is my soul yearning to express? Listen to the answers that arise. Trust them. And then, take one small step in the direction of your inner guidance. And then another. And another.

Key Takeaways:

• Your intuition is a powerful inner guide that can lead you toward your true path. It's a way of knowing that goes beyond logic and reason.

• Learning to listen to your intuition takes practice. Pay attention to your body, create space for silence, journal your insights, and ask yourself what feels right.

• Distinguishing between intuition and impulses can be challenging, but intuition is usually quiet and gentle, while impulses are loud and insistent.

• Trusting your intuition takes courage and a willingness to welcome the unknown.

• Developing your intuition is a process of deepening your connection with yourself and the divine intelligence that flows through all things.

• This journey is about coming home to yourself, recognizing that you are a spiritual being with infinite potential.

~

Chapter 5

BOUNCING BACK

When our hearts are bewitched by Thy smiles and frowns,

Can we gain life from these two alternating states?

The fertile garden of love, as it is boundless,

Contains other fruits besides joy and sorrow.

The true lover is exalted above these two states,

He is fresh and green independently of autumn or spring!

- Rumi

"The wound is the place where the Light enters you."

- Rumi

This quote from Rumi serves as a guiding light for this chapter. It suggests that our struggles, our pain, our setbacks—these are not simply obstacles to be overcome, but rather opportunities for growth, for transformation, for allowing the light of wisdom and resilience to enter us.

Life has a way of throwing curveballs, doesn't it? Just when you think you've got everything figured out, something unexpected happens that knocks you off your feet. It could be a job loss, a relationship breakup, a health crisis, or any number of challenges that life throws our way. These setbacks can leave us feeling defeated, discouraged, and questioning our own strength.

But what if these challenges, these apparent setbacks, are actually opportunities in disguise? What if, within every challenge, we discover hidden strengths that lead to remarkable personal growth and positive revolution? This chapter is about resilience, the ability to bounce back from adversity, to convert challenges into stepping stones, setbacks into setups for something even greater.

Reframing Perspectives

The first step in converting challenges into growth is to reframe your perspective. This involves shifting your mindset from one of victimhood to one of empowerment. Instead of seeing yourself as a passive recipient of life's misfortunes, you begin to see yourself as an active participant in your own story. You recognize that you have the power to choose how you respond to adversity. You can choose to let the waves toss you around, or you can adjust your sails and steer your ship through the rough waters.

Reframing is about choosing to see challenges not as roadblocks, but as detours, as opportunities to learn, grow, and become stronger. For example, losing a job could be reframed as an opportunity to finally pursue that passion project you've always dreamed of. A relationship ending could be seen as a chance to rediscover yourself and what you truly want in a partner. Even a health crisis could be viewed as a wake-up call to prioritize your well-being and make necessary lifestyle changes. It is about recognizing that you are not defined by your circumstances, but by how you respond to them.

However, it's essential to acknowledge that this reframing takes time. It's not about instantly finding the "silver lining" in every situation, especially when you're surrounded by pain. Sometimes, you simply need to allow yourself to feel the difficult emotions—the sadness, the anger, the fear. It's okay to grieve a loss, to mourn what could have been. As we learned in earlier chapters, mindfulness can be a powerful tool here. Allowing yourself to fully experience and process these emotions, without judgment, is a crucial part of healing and moving forward. Trying to force a positive perspective too soon can be counterproductive and may even invalidate your genuine feelings.

Once you've given yourself space to feel, you can then begin to explore different perspectives. It's often said that hindsight is 20/20. When we look back on our past challenges, we can often see how they shaped us, and how they led us to where we are today. We can see the lessons we learned, the strength we gained, and the growth that occurred as a result. But what if we could develop that kind of perspective during the actual challenge? What if we could learn to see the potential for growth even as we're going through difficult times?

This is where the practice of self-reflection comes in. Taking the time to journal, meditate, or simply contemplate your experiences can help you gain a deeper understanding of what you're going through and what you're learning.

Ask yourself:

- What is this situation teaching me?

- What strengths am I developing as a result of this challenge?

- How can I use this experience to help others?

- What is the bigger picture here?

- Could there be a purpose behind this pain?

These questions can help you shift your focus from the problem to the potential, from the pain to the purpose.

Adversity, while painful, can be a powerful catalyst for growth and transformation. It can force you to confront your deepest fears, to question your beliefs, and to re-evaluate your priorities. It can strip away the superficial and reveal what truly matters. Think of a diamond. It's formed under immense pressure, deep within the earth. Without that pressure, it would just be a lump of coal. Similarly, it's often through the pressures of life that we are remolded into something stronger, more beautiful, and more resilient.

Rumi understood that adversity is not merely something to be endured, but something to be appreciated as a catalyst for transformation. He illustrates this beautifully in his seemingly simple story of 'The Chickpeas'.

On market day, a woman went shopping and came back with a big bag of chickpeas, which she intended to use to make several kinds of salad, dip, and soup. She cleaned the chickpeas, rinsing them well and then soaking them for several hours before boiling them slowly in a big cauldron.

As soon as the pot began to boil, the chickpeas started bouncing up and down, screaming; "You've bought us, we're yours, why set us on fire now?"

"It's time for you to boil, so stay quiet and be patient. I must cook you properly until you're ready to be added to my best dishes," she asserted knowingly. "When you were growing in the fields you were amply nourished, but now it's time to put up with some hardship. You know that your ultimate purpose is to become nourishment for the spirit, not just the body! That's how in the end you'll reap your greatest rewards."

The chickpeas slowly stopped bouncing around and quieted down, resigned to the fact that if they wanted to be part of the grand scheme of life, they would have to forfeit their material existence and trust in the guidance of their mistress.

Imagine, for a moment, the chickpeas in the pot. The boiling water, the intense heat, represents the challenges, the hardships, the 'curveballs' that life throws our way. These trials, like the boiling water, can feel unbearable, painful, and we, like the chickpeas, may cry out in protest, questioning why we must endure such suffering. But the woman, who represents a higher wisdom, a divine perspective, explains that this distress is necessary. It's through this 'boiling' that the chickpeas are transformed, becoming soft, palatable, and capable of fulfilling their purpose. Similarly, it is often through our trials that we are softened, shaped, and made ready for a greater purpose. The chickpeas' ultimate purpose is to nourish, not just the body, but the spirit. This suggests that the challenges we face are not meant to destroy us, but to refine us, to prepare us for a higher level of being. Just as the chickpeas become nourishing food, we, too, can emerge from our trials stronger, wiser, and more capable of fulfilling our own unique purpose.

The chickpeas eventually surrender to the process, trusting in the wisdom of the woman. This highlights the importance of surrendering to a higher power, trusting that even during adversity, there is a plan at work, a purpose unfolding. When we face our own 'boiling points,' our own moments of intense difficulty, we can ponder on the lesson of the chickpeas. We can choose to resist, to cry out in protest, or we can choose to surrender, to trust that this process, however painful, is ultimately life-changing. This doesn't mean passively accepting suffering, but rather actively engaging with our challenges, learning from them, and allowing them to shape us into something stronger, more resilient, and more aligned with our true purpose. Like the chickpeas, we, too, can emerge renewed from the fires of adversity, ready to nourish not only ourselves but also the world around us.

This is the alchemy of resilience: turning the lead of adversity into the gold of growth and transformation. Even in the most dire of circumstances, you have the power to choose your attitude, your perspective, your response.

Rumi beautifully captured the idea of finding treasure in ruin when he wrote: "Where there is ruin, there is hope for a treasure." Your struggles, your setbacks, your disappointments—they are not the end of your story. They are simply chapters in a much larger narrative. And within those chapters, if you look closely enough, you will find the seeds of hope, the seeds of growth, the seeds of a brighter future.

Within the Quran, there is a significant emphasis placed on the virtues of patience and perseverance, particularly about the challenges and hardships that one may encounter in life.

"And We will surely test you with something of fear and hunger and a loss of wealth and lives and fruits, but give good tidings to the patient, Who, when disaster strikes them, say, 'Indeed we belong to Allah, and indeed to Him we will return.'"

(Surah Al-Baqarah, 2:155-156)

This verse reminds us that life's challenges are tests of our patience and strength. By cultivating patience and faith, we can navigate difficult times and ultimately be rewarded with unexpected and extraordinary gifts.

The Prophet Muhammad (peace be upon him) said,

"Amazing is the affair of the believer, verily all of his affair is good, and this is not for no one except the believer. If something of good/happiness befalls him, he is grateful, and that is good for him. If something of harm befalls him, he is patient, and that is good for him." (Sahih Muslim 2999)

This hadith encourages us to view both good and bad times as opportunities for growth and to respond with gratitude and patience.

Imam Al-Ghazali said,

"Do not think of your tribulations as punishments. See them as opportunities to turn back to God, to strengthen your faith, and to refine your character. Every hardship is a chance

to draw closer to your Creator and to discover the resilience within you."

Be Resilient

Resilience is not something you're born with; it's something you develop over time. It's like a muscle that gets stronger with use. The more you face challenges and overcome them, the more resilient you become. Building resilience is an activity, and it starts with believing in yourself and your ability to navigate difficult times.

Here are some practical ways to build your resilience:

- **Cultivate self-compassion.** Treat yourself with the same kindness and compassion that you would offer a close friend. Acknowledge your pain and struggles without judgment. Remind yourself that it's okay to not be okay and that you're doing the best you can.

- **Practice gratitude.** Focusing on what you're grateful for, even during difficulty, can shift your perspective and boost your resilience.

- **Develop a growth mindset.** Welcome challenges as opportunities for learning and growth. See setbacks as temporary and believe in your ability to overcome them. Remind yourself of past challenges you've overcome and the strengths you've developed along the way.

- **Build a support system.** Connect with people who love and support you. Don't be afraid to ask for help when you need it. Sharing your struggles with trusted friends, family, or a therapist can provide valuable perspective and emotional support.

- **Take care of your physical health.** Exercise, eat well, get enough sleep, and avoid harmful substances. Your physical health has a direct impact on your mental and emotional well-being.

- **Find meaning and purpose.** Connect with something greater than yourself. This could be your faith, your values, your passions, or your relationships. Having a sense of purpose can give you the strength to keep going even when things get tough.

- **Practice mindfulness.** As we learned in previous chapters, paying attention to the present moment without judgment can help you regulate your emotions and reduce stress. Mindfulness can be especially helpful when facing difficult emotions, allowing you to observe them without getting swept away by them.

- **Learn from your mistakes.** Don't dwell on your failures, but learn from them. See them as valuable lessons that can help you grow and improve. Ask yourself: "What can I do differently next time?"

- **Seek professional help.** If you are dealing with significant trauma or mental health issues, consider seeking professional guidance. Therapists can offer tools and techniques to move forward.

- **Focus on what you can control.** Instead of worrying about things you can't change, focus your energy on what you can control: your thoughts, your actions, and your responses.

- **Cultivate self-belief.** Remind yourself of your strengths, your past successes, and your inherent worth. Develop a deep trust in your ability to handle whatever life throws your way. This can be fostered through positive self-talk, affirmations, and celebrating your accomplishments, no matter how small.

- **Foster courage.** Courage is not the absence of fear, but the willingness to act despite it. Take small steps outside your comfort zone, gradually building your confidence and your capacity to face challenges head-on. Each time you face a fear, no matter how small, you reinforce your resilience and your belief in yourself.

Building resilience is a process of continuous growth and self-discovery. By incorporating these practices into your daily life, you'll not only be better equipped to handle life's challenges but also cultivate a deeper sense of inner strength, peace, and fulfillment.

The journey of converting challenges into growth is not a linear one. It's a winding path with ups and downs, twists and turns. There will be moments of clarity and moments of confusion. There will be times when you feel strong and times when you feel weak. That's okay. The main thing is to keep moving forward, one step at a time. Have faith; even if the road ahead is unclear, your destiny has a meaning. Trust that the challenges you face are not meant to break you, but to make you stronger.

Key Takeaways:

• Reframing your perspective can help you shift from a mindset of victimhood to one of empowerment.

• Adversity can be a powerful catalyst for growth, forcing you to confront your fears and re-evaluate your priorities.

• You always have a choice in how you respond to adversity.

• Self-reflection can help you gain a deeper understanding of your experiences and what you're learning.

• Resilience is a skill that can be developed over time.

• Challenges are opportunities for growth and transformation.

~

Chapter 6

FREE YOURSELF

Every night spirits are released from this cage,

And set free, neither lording it nor lorded over.

At night prisoners are unaware of their prison,

At night kings are unaware of their majesty.

Then there is no thought or care for loss or gain,

No regard to such an one or such an one.

- Rumi

"Stop acting so small. You are the universe in ecstatic motion."

- Rumi

These powerful words of Rumi touch the core of our life's truth. It's an invitation to step into our greatness, to let go of the limitations we place on ourselves, and to cherish the flow of life. We've walked together through the noisy marketplace of the mind, learned to calm the storms of anxiety, discovered the wisdom that resides in the present moment, and started to trust that quiet inner voice, that compass of the soul. We've learned to cope with adversity with strength. Now, we arrive at a critical point in our journey: learning the art of letting go.

This chapter is about releasing the tight grip of control we often try to maintain over our lives, especially our thoughts, and finding freedom in surrender. Because the truth is, overthinking often stems from a deep-seated need to control everything. And that's a recipe for exhaustion and a lot of unnecessary suffering.

Think about it: why do we overthink? Why do we replay conversations in our heads, analyze every possible outcome of a decision, or worry about things that haven't even happened yet? At the root of it all is often a desire for control. We believe that if we can just think hard enough, plan meticulously enough, or anticipate every possible scenario, we can somehow control the outcome and avoid pain, disappointment, or failure.

It's a natural human instinct, this desire for control. We want to feel safe, secure, and certain about our lives. But here's the hard truth: life is inherently uncertain. We can't control everything, no matter how hard we try. And the more we try to force things into a neat little box, the more anxious and overwhelmed we often become. It's like trying to hold onto water—the tighter you squeeze, the more it slips through your fingers.

Overthinking is like being trapped in a mental maze. You go round and round, exploring every possible path, but you never seem to find your way out. You become so focused on analyzing every detail, every potential problem, that you lose sight of the bigger picture. You become paralyzed by indecision, unable to move forward because you're too busy second-guessing yourself. This over-analysis can be incredibly draining, both mentally and emotionally. It depletes your energy, steals your joy, and prevents you from experiencing the present moment. It's like being stuck in a mental prison of your own making. And the worst part is, the more you overthink, the more anxious you become, which leads to more overthinking. It's a vicious cycle that can be incredibly difficult to break.

So, how do we break free from this cycle? How do we learn to let go of the need to control everything? The answer lies in the wisdom of surrender. Now, surrender doesn't mean giving up or becoming passive. It doesn't mean that you stop caring or that you stop pursuing your goals. It simply means accepting that there are some things in life that you cannot control, and that's okay. Surrendering means having faith in a greater design. It's about letting go of your need to have all the answers and grasping the unknown with a sense of faith and openness. It's like being in a river. You can fight against the current, exhausting yourself and getting nowhere, or you can relax, let go, and allow the river to carry you.

But before we can truly espouse surrender, it's helpful to understand what's driving our need for control in the first place. Often, it's fear. Fear of the unknown, fear of failure, fear of not being good enough, fear of being hurt, fear of losing what we have. These fears can create a deep-seated anxiety that fuels our overthinking and makes it difficult to let go. We think that if we can just control every variable, we can somehow protect ourselves from pain and disappointment. But the truth is, this need for control is an illusion. It's a way of trying to create a false sense of security in an inherently uncertain world. And it often ends up causing us more suffering in the long run.

Rumi expressed this beautifully when he said: "Be like a tree and let the dead leaves drop." This line speaks to the heart of surrender. This is about recognizing your own inherent power and beauty, and letting go of the things that no longer serve you. Just as a tree naturally sheds its leaves in the autumn, we too must learn to release the thoughts, beliefs, and attachments that are weighing us down.

Let's try a simple visualization exercise to help you practice letting go:

- Find a comfortable position, either sitting or lying down. Close your eyes if you wish, and take a few deep breaths.

- Now, imagine yourself holding a balloon in each hand. Each balloon represents something you're trying to control, something you're worried about, or something from the past that you're holding onto. It could be a relationship, a job, a fear, a regret, anything at all.

- Visualize yourself opening your hands and releasing the balloons. Watch them as they float up into the sky, getting smaller and smaller until they disappear. As you release each balloon, feel yourself becoming lighter, freer.

- Another visualization you can try is imagining yourself standing by a riverbank. See your worries, fears, and attachments as leaves floating on the surface of the water. Watch as the current carries them away, downstream and out of sight. With each leaf that floats away, feel yourself letting go a little more.

Here are some practical, actionable steps you can start implementing right away to cultivate the art of letting go:

- **Identify your control triggers:** What are the situations, people, or thoughts that tend to trigger your need to control? Keep a journal for a week, noting down when you feel the urge to control or when you find yourself overthinking. This will help you become more aware of your patterns.

- **Challenge your need for certainty:** Ask yourself, "Do I really need to know how this will turn out? Can I be okay with not knowing?" Practice tolerating uncertainty, even in small ways. Start by making a small decision without overthinking it. For example, choose a restaurant for dinner without reading countless reviews.

• **Focus on what you can control:** You can't control other people's actions or the outcome of every situation. But you can control your own thoughts, your actions, and your responses. Make a list of things that are within your control and things that are not. Focus your energy on the former.

• **Practice acceptance:** Accept that life is full of uncertainties, imperfections, and things you cannot change. Acceptance doesn't mean resignation; it means acknowledging reality as it is, without resistance. When you encounter a difficult situation, acknowledge your feelings about it, and then remind yourself that you can't change what has happened. Instead, focus on how you can respond constructively.

• **Cultivate trust:** Trust that there is a higher power or a larger plan at work, even if you can't see it. This could be God, the Universe, or simply the natural flow of life. Reflect on times in the past when things worked out for the best, even though you couldn't see it at the time. This can help you build trust in the unfolding of your life.

• **Accept imperfection:** Let go of the need for everything to be perfect. Perfectionism is a major driver of overthinking and anxiety. Accept your imperfections and allow yourself to make mistakes. Practice self-compassion and remind yourself that you're doing the best you can.

- **Practice mindfulness:** Bring your attention back to the present moment whenever you find yourself getting lost in thoughts about the past or the future. Use your breath as an anchor. Remember the mindfulness exercises we discussed in earlier chapters? Use them throughout your day to stay grounded in the present moment. They can be especially helpful when you feel yourself getting caught up in overthinking.

- **Set intentions, not expectations:** Instead of setting rigid expectations, set intentions. Intentions are about the direction you want to go, while expectations are about specific outcomes. For example, instead of expecting a specific outcome from a job interview, set the intention to do your best and be open to whatever happens.

- **Learn to say no:** Saying "no" to things that drain your energy or don't align with your values is a powerful way to set boundaries and protect your peace of mind. Practice saying "no" to requests that you don't feel comfortable with or that you simply don't have time for.

- **Practice the "Serenity Prayer":** "God, grant me the serenity to accept the things I cannot change, the courage to change the things I can, and the wisdom to know the difference." This simple prayer encapsulates the essence of surrender, acceptance, and discernment. Use it as a daily reminder to focus on what you can control and to let go of the rest.

All of these practical steps play a crucial role in learning to let go. Mindfulness helps you stay present and not get swept away by your thoughts. Grounding techniques anchor you in your body and the present moment when anxiety and overthinking threaten to take over. And your intuition, that inner compass we discussed in Chapter 4, can guide you toward making decisions that are aligned with your true self, helping you release the need for external control. By integrating these practices into your daily life, you create a strong foundation for letting go and surrendering to the flow of life.

Rumi, with his deep insights into the human condition, uses metaphors to explain the power of surrender. One of his most beautiful and evocative metaphors is found in the story of 'The Reed Flute's Song'.

A reed flute was once heard lamenting in beautiful, melancholic tones. Someone asked the flute, "Why do you cry so sorrowfully? What is the source of your pain?"

The flute replied, "I was once a reed growing tall and green in the reed bed, connected to my roots and nourished by the water. But then I was cut, separated from my source, and fashioned into a flute. My heart was hollowed out, and now, every breath that passes through me becomes a song of longing, a yearning to return to my original state, to be one with the Reed Bed again."

The song of the reed flute serves as a metaphor for the journey of the human soul. We are all, like the reed flute, separated from our Source, from the Divine. And it is this separation that causes us pain and longing. Our ego, like the flute maker, tries to shape us into something we are not, to control our path. But true fulfillment comes not from resisting our nature, but from surrendering to the Divine will, from allowing the breath of the Beloved to flow through us and create a beautiful melody.

The reed flute does not resist the breath that passes through it, nor does it try to control the tune that is played. It simply allows itself to be an instrument, a vessel for the music of the Divine. And in that surrender, it finds its true purpose and creates a sound that touches the hearts of all who hear it. This is the essence of surrender, to let go of our own will and to become an instrument for the will of the Beloved.

The reed flute's lament is a powerful symbol of the human condition. We, too, often feel a sense of separation, a longing for something more, a yearning for connection with our Source. The flute's surrender to being played, to being an instrument of the Divine breath, represents the essence of spiritual surrender. It's about letting go of our ego's desire to control and allowing ourselves to be guided by a higher power. The beautiful melody produced by the flute is a metaphor for the beauty and meaning that can emerge in our lives when we surrender to a larger plan. Just as the reed flute finds its purpose in being played, we, too, can find our purpose by aligning ourselves with the Divine will and allowing our lives to be an expression of that higher calling.

We want to know what's going to happen, how things will turn out, and what other people are thinking. But the truth is, we can never know for sure. Life is full of surprises, both good and bad. Welcoming uncertainty can be incredibly liberating. It allows you to let go of the need to control every outcome and to trust that things will work out, even if it's not in the way you expected. It frees you from the burden of trying to predict the future and allows you to focus on the present moment.

Think of it like this: When you're driving a car, you can't see everything that's ahead of you. You can't see around every curve or over every hill. But you trust that the road will continue, and you adjust your driving accordingly. Life is the same way. You can't see what's coming, but you can trust that you have the ability to navigate whatever comes your way.

When you're caught in the grip of overthinking, it's easy to lose perspective. Small problems can seem insurmountable, and minor setbacks can feel like the end of the world. One helpful technique is to practice "zooming out" and looking at the bigger picture. Ask yourself: *"Will this matter in a week? A month? A year? Five years?"* Often, the things we worry about most are relatively insignificant in the grand scheme of things.

The Quran highlights the significance of faith in God's plan:

"And whoever relies upon Allah—then He is sufficient for him. Indeed, Allah will accomplish His purpose. Allah has already set a destiny for everything."

(Surah At-Talaq, 65:3)

This verse reminds us that surrendering to a higher power can bring peace, and that everything happens for a reason.

The Prophet Muhammad (peace be upon him) said,

"If you all depend on Allah with due reliance, He would certainly give you provision as He gives it to birds who go forth hungry in the morning and return with a full belly at dusk." (Jami' at-Tirmidhi 2344)

This hadith encourages us to trust in God's provision and to let go of our anxieties about the future.

Imam Ali stated,

"The biggest weakness is to worry before the trouble comes to you, for you may never be afflicted by it."

This highlights the futility of worrying about things that may never happen and the importance of focusing on the present.

Letting go also means releasing the past. It means forgiving yourself and others for past mistakes and recognizing that you can't change what has already happened. It means choosing to focus on the present moment and the possibilities that lie ahead, rather than dwelling on regrets or resentments. It is a practice. It's something you must consciously choose to do repeatedly until it becomes a habit.

Bear in mind that you are not alone. We are all on this path together, learning and growing as we go. Cherish your greatness, let go of your fears, and keep trust in yourself.

This is a process of unlearning and relearning. It's about unlearning the habits of overthinking, control, and worry, and relearning how to trust, surrender, and flow with life. Understand that your thoughts and emotions don't define you. You are the awareness that observes those thoughts and emotions.

Key Takeaways:

- Overthinking often stems from a need to control.

- Surrender doesn't mean giving up; it means accepting what you can't control and trusting in a larger plan.

- Letting go is a practice that requires conscious effort and patience.

- Techniques like identifying your triggers, challenging your need for certainty, and focusing on what you can control can help you let go.

- Accepting uncertainty can be liberating and free you from the burden of trying to predict the future.

- Gaining perspective by zooming out and looking at the bigger picture can help you manage overthinking.

- Letting go is a journey of self-discovery, trust, and finding peace within yourself.

As we conclude this book, let's carry the wisdom of Rumi with us: "Stop acting so small. You are the universe in ecstatic motion." This is your invitation to step into your greatness, to let go of your limitations, and to cherish the fullness of who you are. You are not meant to be confined by your fears and anxieties. You are meant to soar, to expand, to connect with the infinite possibilities that lie within you.

The process of letting go ultimately leads to a deeper connection with self-love. This means treating yourself with kindness, compassion, and understanding. It's about recognizing that you are worthy of peace, joy, and fulfillment, regardless of your past mistakes or your present circumstances. It is about freeing yourself from the shackles of overthinking and relishing the freedom that comes with surrender. Believe that everything is happening for a reason and that you are where you need to be right now.

This is your invitation to let go, to trust, and to live a beautiful, messy, and perfectly imperfect life. You deserve to be kind to yourself. You're doing the best you can, and that's always enough. It's time to silence that inner critic and amplify the voice of your inner champion. You've got this.

Arise, O son! burst thy bonds and be free!

How long wilt thou be captive to silver and gold?

Though thou pour the ocean into thy pitcher,

It can hold no more than one day's store.

The pitcher of the desire of the covetous never fills,

The oyster-shell fills not with pearls till it is content;

Only he whose garment is rent by the violence of love

Is wholly pure from covetousness and sin.

- Rumi

· · ·~· ·•· ·~· · ·

The Road Ahead

Our shared exploration has reached its end, a journey guided by the wisdom of Rumi and Islamic principles. It's been a path of self-discovery, a move toward finding lasting peace within.

Let's pause and reflect on the key insights we've gathered. You've learned that your thoughts are merely visitors, not permanent residents of your consciousness. You now possess practical tools—mindfulness exercises, grounding techniques, and breathwork—to bring peace to your mind and create space between yourself and your thoughts. We discovered the importance of presence, of being fully immersed in the now, and how gratitude can shift your focus from what's lacking to what's abundant. You began to understand that your intuition is a trustworthy inner guide, a compass pointing toward your most authentic path. And, importantly, we acknowledged that challenges are not merely roadblocks but rather chances for growth, the very places where light enters you, just like Rumi so beautifully stated. You are no longer a captive of overthinking but rather a seeker of inner tranquility.

Throughout this book, you have explored how to handle internal battles. We addressed the all too common struggle of feeling overwhelmed by the ceaseless flow of thoughts, the anxiety that can grip our hearts, and the feeling of disconnect that can leave us feeling lost in the current of life. Now, you stand equipped to face these challenges with newfound resilience and wisdom. You hold the tools to quiet the mental chatter, to navigate difficult emotions, and to trust your inner guidance.

Change is not an abstract concept; it is an attainable reality you can create. As a reader of Rumi, you understand that growth is a continuous exercise of letting go, moving toward the divine, and seeking enlightenment. It involves finding your way to the quiet field where words are unnecessary. Practice the idea that transformation is a series of conscious choices you make each day. By using these tools and weaving them into the fabric of your life, you possess the power to revolutionize your existence.

So, what are your next steps? As you close this book, I encourage you to do the following:

- Commit to a Daily Practice: Dedicate even just a few minutes each day to mindfulness exercises, breathwork, or moments of quiet reflection. Consistency is key.

- Listen to Your Intuition: Take small steps each day to act upon that inner knowing, trusting that it is guiding you toward your true purpose.

- Practice Gratitude: Before getting out of bed each morning, identify three things you're grateful for and keep this practice as a reminder of the good all around you.

- Consider Challenges as Opportunities: When you encounter difficulties, pause, reflect, and see it as a chance to gain wisdom, expand your understanding, and grow stronger.

Keep in mind that the wisdom within these pages is meant to be explored, experienced, and integrated into your unique rhythm of living. It is a path toward freedom, a journey of knowing your own power and potential. Keep seeking, keep learning, keep growing.

May you always find a sense of peace, and joy as you move forward. May the light of wisdom illuminate your path, and may your heart remain open to the vastness of love that is always available. As Rumi wisely reminds us, "Let yourself be silently drawn by the stronger pull of what you really love."

Know that I am grateful for the time we have shared on these pages, for your engagement, and for your willingness to walk this path toward self-discovery. May your life be an embodiment of Rumi's wisdom. Go forth and shine.

- Ahmed Mustafa

About the Author

Hello, my name is Ahmed Mustafa, and like many of you, I'm just a regular person trying to navigate this complex world we live in. I've never considered myself a scholar or an expert, but rather a curious explorer on a journey to understand life a little better.

We live in a time that's incredibly fast-paced and competitive. Everywhere we look, we're encouraged to strive for individual success, to climb the ladder, and to achieve more. It's easy to get caught up in this race, focusing on what we can achieve for ourselves. But during all this striving, I started to notice a disconnect. I realized that despite all the advancements and opportunities around us, many of us still feel a sense of unease, a feeling that something is missing.

What I've come to understand is that despite the competitive landscape of modern society, our core human desires remain the same. We all long for **connection**; to feel loved, understood, and part of something bigger than ourselves. We crave **purpose**; a sense that our lives have meaning and that we're contributing to the world in some way. We seek **security**;

not just financial stability, but also emotional and mental well-being, a feeling of safety and peace within ourselves. And we're constantly searching for a **balance**; a way to pursue our individual dreams while also fulfilling our responsibilities to our families, communities, and the world around us.

These desires, these deep-seated longings, highlight the ongoing struggle many of us face. We live in a world that often prioritizes individual success over communal well-being, and finding our place in it can feel like trying to solve a complicated puzzle. How can we be successful and also be fulfilled? How can we take care of ourselves and also take care of others?

My journey led me to the **wisdom of the East**, particularly the teachings of Rumi and the principles found within Islam. These ancient teachings, though born in a different time and place, resonated deeply with the questions I was asking about modern life. I discovered that they offered thoughtful insights into the human condition, providing guidance on how to find inner peace, heal from past hurts, and build meaningful relationships; the very things that many of us are searching for today.

I'm not here to tell you that I have all the answers. But what I can share is my own exploration of these eternal principles and how they've helped me to better understand myself and the world around me. The books I've written are a reflection of this journey. They are an attempt to bridge the gap between ancient wisdom and modern challenges, to show how the teachings of the East can offer practical solutions to the problems we face in our everyday lives.

My hope is that through these books, you'll find tools and insights that echo with your own experiences, that you'll discover a path towards greater peace, purpose, and connection, and eventually, together, we can create a world that values not just individual success, but also the well-being of us all. Because at the end of the day, we're all in this together, searching for a way to live a life that is both meaningful and fulfilling.

···•·⌐•·•··•·∼·•··

Explore Other
Rumi-Inspired Books

ISBN: 978-1-998843-52-7

ISBN: 978-1-998843-49-7

www.ingramcontent.com/pod-product-compliance
Lightning Source LLC
Chambersburg PA
CBHW031226120626
46545CB00003B/1005